Contents

Energy from matter

Nuclear power comes from the energy stored inside atoms. These are the tiny particles from which everything around us is made.

Atoms are the building blocks of all substances. Every atom has a central part, called a nucleus, which is where the word nuclear comes from. We can use nuclear energy to provide the power to work machines, as well as to light and heat our homes, offices and factories.

The term energy comes from the Greek word *energos*, meaning active or working. Energy sources help other things become active and do work, such as lifting or moving objects. For example, nuclear power can be used to make electricity. So when you switch on an electric light in your home, the energy to make it work might have come from a nuclear power station.

The control room of Calder Hall, in northern England. This became the world's first full-scale nuclear power station in 1956. This photograph was taken a year later.

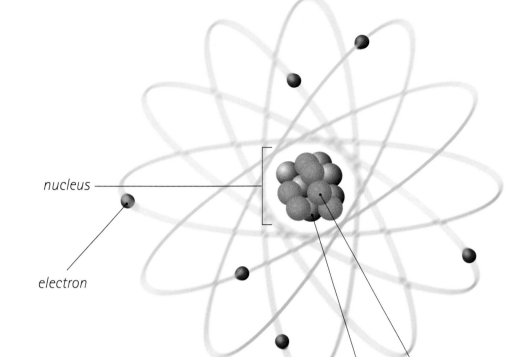

This diagram of the inside of an atom shows the three different kinds of particles.

nucleus

electron

neutron

proton

Inside an atom

The central nucleus of every atom is made up of a cluster of particles called protons and neutrons. Lighter particles, called electrons, circle around the nucleus. The atoms of each of the world's elements – such as carbon, gold, hydrogen, oxygen or uranium – contain a different number of protons. The metal uranium, which is the most important element for nuclear energy, has 92 protons, while hydrogen has just one. But each element can have different numbers of neutrons. The most common form of uranium has 146 neutrons and is called uranium-238 (or U-238 for short), because it has a total of 238 protons and neutrons.

Releasing energy

Some elements have unstable atoms, which means that their nuclei can break apart. When they do so, they give off particles and energy before forming a more stable nucleus. The elements that can go through this process naturally are known as radioactive elements. Uranium is radioactive, and the form known as U-235 (with 92 protons and 143 neutrons) is least stable and releases most energy when its nucleus breaks apart. We produce nuclear power by purposely breaking apart the nuclei of unstable atoms.

NON-RENEWABLE RESOURCE

Nuclear power is not a renewable resource, unlike wind, water, solar, geothermal or biomass power. This is because nuclear fuel is used up to produce power (and the spent fuel is very dangerous). Once we have mined and used all the Earth's uranium, there won't be any more.

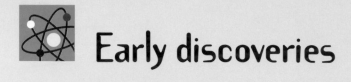

Early discoveries

The French scientist Henri Becquerel discovered radioactivity in 1896. Becquerel found that invisible rays from a lump of uranium ore affected a photographic plate.

His work was carried on by the Polish-born French scientist Marie Curie, together with her husband Pierre. The Curies studied a metallic rock called pitchblende in their search for the source of radiation. Their studies helped them discover two new metallic elements, which they named radium (from the word ray) and polonium (after Poland, Marie's homeland).

These exciting discoveries led to Becquerel and the Curies winning the Nobel Prize for physics in 1903. But scientists still did not fully understand this mysterious radioactivity, and they had little idea of its dangers. Marie Curie herself died of a blood disease that was probably caused by exposure to radiation.

Marie Curie working in her laboratory in Paris in 1905.

The father of nuclear science

At the beginning of the 20th century, scientists still thought that atoms were the smallest particles and that they could not be divided. This changed in 1911, when the New Zealander Ernest Rutherford discovered that atoms have a nucleus. He also found out that the nucleus was surrounded by particles travelling at enormous speeds – electrons. Rutherford's work won him a Nobel Prize, and he is often called the father of nuclear science.

Mass and energy

In 1905 the famous German-born scientist Albert Einstein worked out that the mass (or amount of matter) in atoms can change into energy. Later this led scientists to realize that when a nucleus breaks apart, some of its mass seems to be lost. But it is not really lost – it is changed into energy. And Einstein worked out that the amount of energy released is enormous. Scientists later discovered that one kilogram of radioactive uranium can release more energy than burning three million kilograms of coal.

Using a Geiger counter to measure levels of radiation. Hans Geiger, the German scientist who invented the instrument in 1912, was Ernest Rutherford's assistant.

Albert Einstein (1879–1955) developed many ideas and theories. This photograph was taken in 1931. Nine years later he became an American citizen.

Mining uranium

Uranium is a very heavy, silvery-white metal in the Earth's crust. It has to be extracted from ores obtained from different kinds of rocks.

Uranium was first found in 1789 and was named after the planet Uranus, which had been discovered eight years earlier. The ore was first found in pitchblende rock, which is still the most important source of uraninite, or uranium ore.

Sandstone, shale and granite rocks also sometimes contain uranium. Most of the ore comes from underground mines, where miners dig vertical shafts down from the surface. Horizontal tunnels lead off the shafts to the ore deposits, where miners or remote-control drills remove it in chunks. Some uranium also comes from opencast or open-pit mines, where metal is recovered from thick beds of ore that lie close to the surface.

Trucks carry uranium ore from an opencast mine in New Mexico, USA.

From North America to West Africa

Canadian mines produce more than a quarter of the world's uranium. The world's second biggest producer is Australia, followed by Kazakhstan. Next comes Niger in West Africa, where uranium ore is the country's most important natural resource. Niger exports its uranium, which mainly comes from sandstone rocks and makes up two thirds of the country's income from abroad. Though all these countries are rich in uranium, only Canada has nuclear power stations.

This aerial photograph shows some of the sandstone and uranium deposits in an open-pit mining region of Niger. The country also has underground mines.

HAZARDOUS MATERIAL

U–235 makes up less than 1 per cent of uranium, and this is increased to up to 4 per cent at fuel-enrichment plants. Throughout the whole process of mining and using uranium – called the nuclear fuel cycle – special precautions have to be taken so that people are not exposed to radiation or the dangerous chemicals used in the processes.

A sample of U-235 powder.

Uranium-235

Uranium ore is crushed, ground and treated with chemicals. This produces a substance called yellowcake, which mainly contains the most common isotope (or form) of uranium, U-238. Small amounts of the more useful U-235 are separated so that this isotope is increased. This is a complicated process, and one method involves spinning the material round very fast in a machine called a centrifuge.

Generating electricity

Nuclear power stations generate about one sixth of the world's electricity. Just like coal-fired plants, they use energy to create heat and produce steam to drive a generator.

Rather than burning fuel, a nuclear reactor (see pages 14–15) uses a chain reaction of splitting nuclei to create the heat energy needed to boil water. Special precautions are taken to make sure that all radioactivity stays within the reactor, which stands inside a metre-thick concrete and steel structure called a containment building. This is often dome-shaped.

Nuclear power stations need a great deal of water, both to make steam and to cool the system, which is why they are usually built near the sea, lakes or rivers. The electricity generated is carried along power cables to towns and cities. The cables are often held high above the ground on tall pylons.

This French nuclear power station stands near the River Loire.

Turbines and generators

The idea of generating electricity began in 1831, when the British scientist Michael Faraday discovered that he could create electricity by moving a magnet through a coil of copper wire. This led to the invention of the generator, which works by changing mechanical energy into electrical energy.

In a nuclear power station, the power of high-pressure steam provides mechanical energy by hitting the blades of a turbine and turning them. The blades are connected to a shaft, which is also attached to a generator. Inside the generator, the shaft makes magnets spin inside wire coils to produce electricity.

In the control room

All the operations in a nuclear power plant are monitored in a central control room. Many operations are fully automated, but experienced controllers constantly check that everything is happening exactly as it should.

If there is an emergency, computers shut down the reactors and other equipment, and it is impossible to overrule them. Today, many nuclear-power companies have simulators, so that operators can practise controlling a power plant. The simulators are like those used by airline pilots, and nuclear engineers can also practise what to do in an emergency.

These turbines are driven by the steam from a reactor in a Californian nuclear power station.

Nuclear reactors

The central structure of a nuclear power station is the reactor, and inside it is the reactor core.

The core contains nuclear fuel, which is made up of metal rods containing pellets of uranium. These are surrounded by a liquid or gas that carries heat away to boil water and make steam. Some reactors use water as a coolant; others use carbon dioxide gas.

In the reactor core, the nuclear fuel releases neutrons that break other nuclei and start a chain reaction. Control rods are inserted into the core to slow down the reaction. The rods are usually made of boron, which absorbs neutrons. The rods can be moved in and out of the core, slowing down or speeding up the nuclear reaction. A separate set of shutdown rods can be inserted into the core to stop the reactions quickly if there is an emergency.

The four reactors of the Paluel power station on the coast of northern France are contained in domes. They are connected to turbine and generator buildings. This power station opened in 1985.

Pressurized water

There are several different kinds of nuclear reactors, though they work in a similar way. More than half of those operating in the world are pressurized water reactors (or PWRs for short).

Inside the PWR containment building, the reactor heats water under great pressure, which allows it to get hotter than normal before it boils. Heat from this water boils different water in a steam generator. The high-pressure water is pumped back to the reactor, where it is heated up again. Steam drives the plant's turbine, before cooling, changing back into water and returning to the steam generator.

Fast breeder

There are a few experimental fast-breeder reactors in the world. They get their name because they 'breed' or make more nuclear fuel as they react. They are called fast because they do not slow down neutrons. Other kinds of reactors do this to make the particles more effective at breaking nuclei.

This diagram of a pressurized water reactor shows that the two water systems are separate.

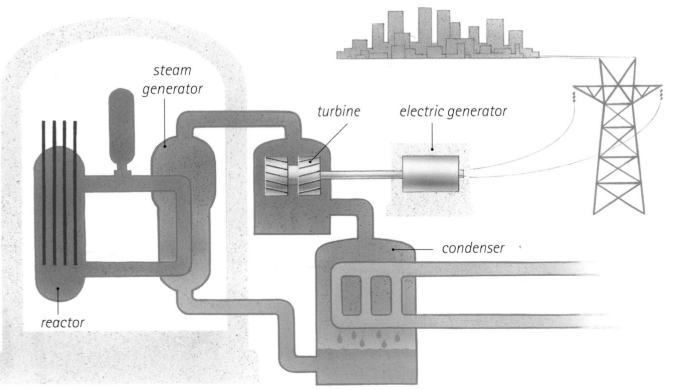

steam generator

turbine   electric generator

condenser

reactor

Destructive weapons

The first nuclear weapons of the 1940s were atom bombs. These worked by creating nuclear fission and allowing a huge chain reaction to take place.

On the ground a shock wave was followed by a fireball and then radioactive fallout. American warplanes dropped two atom bombs on Japan in 1945, with devastating results.

The next weapons were H-bombs (hydrogen bombs), in which the nuclei of hydrogen atoms were forced together. These fusion bombs were even more destructive than fission bombs, and many of today's nuclear weapons work this way.

As well as bombs, some modern armies have nuclear missiles, mines and torpedoes. An international agreement called a non-proliferation treaty aims to stop nuclear weapons becoming more widespread and works towards nuclear disarmament. Five countries that have

A mushroom cloud towers up to 6000 metres over Nagasaki, on 9 August 1945. Japan surrendered five days later, ending the Second World War.

Japanese schoolchildren walk past the Memorial Dome in Hiroshima. Those who died in the city are remembered every year on 6 August, Hiroshima Day.

nuclear weapons have signed the treaty – Britain, China, France, Russia and the United States – and 182 others. A few countries, such as India, North Korea and Pakistan, have declared that they have nuclear weapons, but have not signed the treaty.

Hiroshima

At 8.15 on the morning of 6 August 1945, an American B-29 bomber dropped an atom bomb on the Japanese city of Hiroshima. When the bomb reached a height of 560 metres above the city, an explosive inside it drove one piece of uranium-235 into a larger piece.

The massive nuclear blast killed up to 100,000 people, injuring many more and destroying about 13 square kilometres of the city. The heat from the blast was so strong that it burned everything in its way, including people. Three days later a plutonium bomb was dropped on Nagasaki, with similarly devastating effects.

Modern missiles

Nuclear missiles are made up of a rocket with one or more explosive sections called warheads. They are guided by on-board computers, and large missiles can travel many thousands of kilometres. Some have been specially developed to be launched from submarines, which are difficult to detect or follow as they move beneath the world's oceans.

The Americans test a nuclear missile off the coast of Florida.

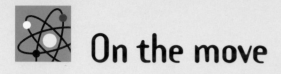

On the move

During the 1950s people believed that nuclear power could be used to drive all sorts of vessels and vehicles.

Nuclear power was first (and most successfully) used in submarines. The power system was very similar to that of a nuclear power station. In a nuclear submarine, a reactor produces steam to drive a turbine that turns a propeller shaft and pushes the vessel through the water.

Unlike other systems, a nuclear engine needs no air and uses very little fuel. One kilogram of uranium produces more energy than 21 million litres of diesel oil. A nuclear submarine can stay underwater for a very long time. In 1960 the twin-reactor *USS Triton* remained submerged for 84 days as it travelled all the way around the world. Nuclear engines are also used for icebreaker ships.

This is how the future looked in 1958. The Ford Nucleon concept car was designed to be powered by its own self-contained nuclear reactor. The dangers of nuclear power meant that it never took to the road.

USS Nautilus

The first nuclear-powered submarine, *Nautilus*, was launched in 1954. On its early voyages *Nautilus* broke all records for time and distance travelled underwater. Then in 1958 it made a historic voyage to the North Pole, where it arrived beneath the ice with a crew of 116 men on board. On the voyage *Nautilus* travelled under the frozen polar ice cap of the Arctic Sea for nearly 3000 kilometres. *Nautilus* went on breaking records for 25 years, before being turned into a museum on the Thames River in Connecticut.

USS Nautilus *was 97 metres long and 8 metres wide.*

Space travel

Many deep-space probes have been powered by small nuclear devices called radioisotope generators. Apollo lunar astronauts also used such generators to power scientific instruments on the Moon.

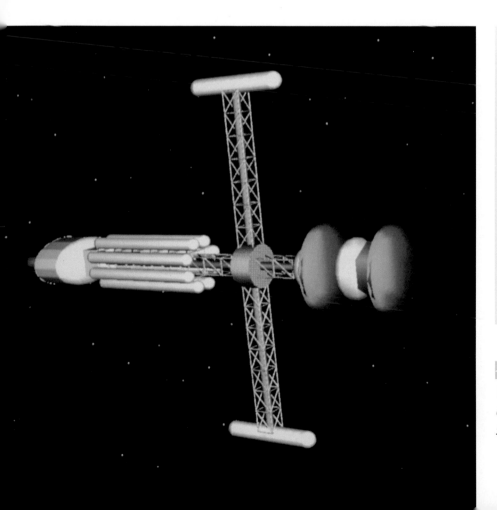

FASTER THROUGH SPACE

American space engineers are working on nuclear-powered unmanned spacecraft, which they hope will visit some of the icy moons of the planet Jupiter. In future, nuclear power could be used by humans to travel to Mars. Burning rocket fuel, the journey would take six months. Nuclear fuel could cut the space journey to two months.

This illustration shows a possible future Mars spacecraft.

Nuclear fusion

Nuclear fusion (meaning uniting or joining together) is the opposite of fission. Fusion occurs when the nuclei of two light atoms combine to form a heavier one.

For fusion to happen, the nuclei must be moving at a very high speed and this requires an extremely high temperature. This is the process that powers the stars. Fusion is called a thermonuclear reaction, and this is what takes place inside an H-bomb (see page 18).

The fusion of 1 kilogram of light nuclei releases more energy than burning 18 million kilograms of coal. Because of this, a lot of research has been carried out into producing a fusion reactor that could generate electricity. Nuclear engineers have built several test reactors, but so far they have not proved practical.

These men are building a test fusion reactor called a tokamak. The Russian name means doughnut-shaped chamber. This reactor can produce a temperature of 510 million °C.

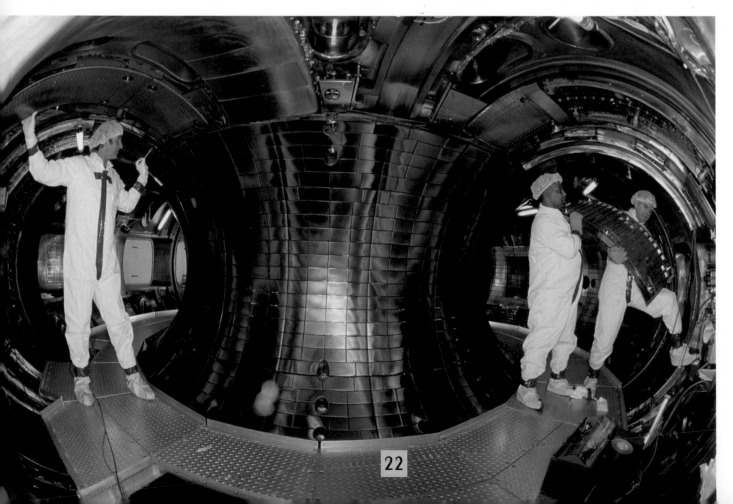

Energy of the stars

All the stars we see in the night sky are huge, hot balls of gas that give out light and heat. We see the light as twinkling pinpoints. New stars are being born all the time, and their energy is produced by nuclear fusion. The same is true of our very own star, the Sun, which gives us all the energy we need to survive on Earth.

At the centre of the Sun, in its core, the high temperature (about 15 million°C) and density (about 100 times the density of water) cause the nuclei of hydrogen atoms to combine to form the nucleus of a helium atom. At the same time, an enormous amount of energy is given off, and this takes just over eight minutes to travel through space and reach us on Earth.

New stars are being formed by nuclear fusion in this spiral galaxy. The photograph was taken from the Hubble space telescope.

Laser technology

Scientists at a laboratory in California used a powerful laser-driven reactor to produce fusion. The huge laser, called Nova, operated from 1985 to 1999. It produced pulses of laser light, which travelled in beams down ten long tubular arms and were then concentrated on a single 1-mm spot. An incredible amount of power in the form of light and heat was concentrated on nuclear fuel for just a billionth of a second, which was long enough to cause nuclei to fuse.

The operators in the middle show the size of the Nova laser device, at the Livermore National Laboratory. Altogether, the laser was as long as a football field.

Around the world

The production and use of nuclear-powered electricity vary greatly around the world. More than 400 nuclear reactors generate electricity in about 30 countries.

More power stations are planned and being built in some places, while others have reached the end of their useful lives and are being shut down. At the beginning of the 21st century, Europe produces well over 40 per cent of the world's nuclear power. North America generates less than a third, and Asia about a quarter of the world total. There is only one nuclear power station on the continent of Africa (in South Africa), just three in South America and none at all in Australia. The United States is the leading national producer of nuclear power, followed by France and Japan.

Power cables carry electricity from the two reactors of the Diablo Canyon power plant on the Pacific coast of California. Nuclear power generates a fifth of US electricity.

INTERNATIONAL CONCERNS

Iran plans to open a nuclear reactor, and in 2005 Russia agreed to supply the Iranians with help and nuclear fuel. The USA and other countries were concerned about this, because they were afraid that Iran might use the fuel to build nuclear weapons.

Workers in anti-radiation suits inspect equipment at a plant in southern France.

Europe

Belgium, France, Lithuania, Slovakia and Sweden – all European countries – use nuclear power to generate more than half of their electricity. In France the figure is more than three quarters, which means that the country depends heavily on its 59 reactors. The French government decided to build many more nuclear plants after the world oil crisis in the 1970s. At the same time French scientists have done a great deal of work to improve nuclear technology. France also exports some of its electricity to other countries, including Italy, which has no nuclear plants.

Increasing production

Many new reactors are planned in several Asian countries. Japan is by far the biggest producer, followed by South Korea, where a further eight reactors are planned in addition to the 20 already producing electricity.

Benefits and problems

One of the advantages of nuclear power is that it produces a huge amount of energy from a small amount of fuel.

Nuclear fuel lasts much longer than coal, natural gas or oil. Another advantage over fossil fuels is that nuclear processes do not release carbon dioxide and so do not pollute the air or add to the problems of global warming. But there are big disadvantages, too. The two most important are the problems of waste and possible accidents.

Many people think that these minus points outweigh the plus points and that nuclear power simply has too many dangers. Another worry is the link with nuclear weapons, and the possibility that terrorists or dictators might get hold of nuclear material and use it for the wrong purpose.

You can see the control rods (see page 14) in the cooling pool of this nuclear reactor. The technology works well, but is it too dangerous?

THE PROBLEM OF WASTE

After it has been used in a power plant, nuclear fuel is much more radioactive than it was before. The material may remain radioactive for hundreds or thousands of years. So it is important to dispose of it safely, but where? At the moment, most spent fuel is stored at or near nuclear plants. Some may be reprocessed and reused, but this is very dangerous. Most experts believe that the best long-term solution is to bury the waste deep underground, in places where there is no danger of earthquakes or floods. Today some nuclear waste is still sent to other countries by ship or train, causing protest from people who say this is extremely risky.

These drums are filled with nuclear waste before being buried in underground trenches. The symbol stands for radioactive.

These demonstrators in Germany protest about plans for a new nuclear power station.

China syndrome

Many people are very concerned about the dangers of nuclear plants. The greatest fear is that a reactor might reach a point known as meltdown and that nuclear fuel might burn through its protective building. In the 1970s this led to a new term, China syndrome, which suggested that a reactor core might burn its way right through the Earth from the USA to China. There was a film of the same title in 1979. Nuclear experts consider this to be impossible, but no one can ignore the potential dangers.

Future trends

During the second half of the 20th century many experts believed that more and more people would use nuclear power all over the world.

Today, the situation appears very different. Some nations are planning to build more reactors, but others are shutting them down and banning further development. At the same time, demand for electricity goes on increasing and environmentalists point out the pollution problems of power stations burning fossil fuels.

A RISK WORTH TAKING?

Are the benefits of nuclear power worth the risks? Many feel that more effort should be put into renewable energy sources, such as wind and water, and their use will surely increase in future. People must also learn to use energy more wisely and sparingly, as scientists go on looking for new ways to exploit the world's energy sources.

A patient is treated in a linear accelerator. This produces high-energy radiation to treat cancer.

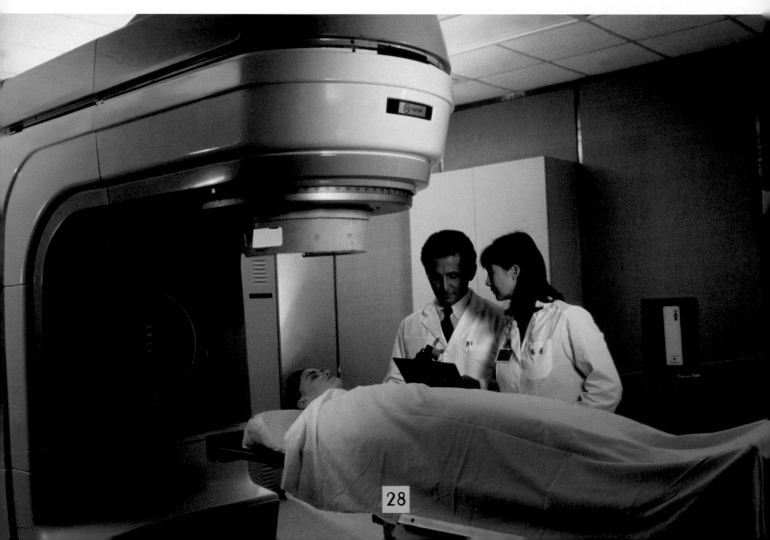

Nuclear medicine

This branch of medicine may develop new techniques in the near future. Today, specialists can use radioactive materials to detect and treat certain diseases. Patients may be given tiny amounts of a radioactive substance, which shows up inside the body on special scanners. In radiotherapy, cancer cells are attacked by X-rays or particles of radium or other radioactive substances. New machines are being invented that are more precise, and perhaps these will be even more effective later this century.

Weapons of mass destruction

Many countries have signed agreements not to build more nuclear weapons (see page 18), not to make any at all or not to test new weapons.

Many environmentalists and peace protesters would like to see all nuclear weapons destroyed, and they will go on working towards this in future. Everyone knows that a nuclear war would have disastrous consequences for our planet. The possible link with weapons also stops many people supporting the production of nuclear fuel. This debate will continue to be vitally important in future.

This underground nuclear test site in Nevada was photographed in the 1960s. International agreements can ban such tests throughout the world in future.

29

Glossary

anomaly An event that is different from normal.

atom The basic particle of all matter.

atom bomb (or atomic bomb) A device that releases explosive, destructive power created by the fission of substances such as uranium-235 and plutonium-239.

chain reaction A series of continuing reactions (such as nuclear fission) in which each one causes the next.

containment building (or structure) A strong, often dome-shaped structure containing a nuclear reactor.

control rod A rod that absorbs neutrons and can be put into a nuclear reactor to slow down fission.

core The central part of a nuclear reactor.

electron A particle in an atom, which circles the nucleus. It has a negative electric charge.

element A substance that cannot be separated into a simpler form.

environmentalist A person who is concerned about and acts to protect the natural environment.

fallout Radioactive dust created by a nuclear explosion.

fast breeder A nuclear reactor in which neutrons are not slowed down and nuclear fuel is produced as it reacts.

fission Splitting an atomic nucleus.

fuel enrichment Increasing the amount of a more radioactive isotope in nuclear fuel such as uranium.

fusion Joining together atomic nuclei.

Geiger counter An instrument that measures radiation.

generator A machine that turns mechanical energy into electrical energy.